CHARLIE RUSSELL

TALE-TELLING COWBOY ARTIST

Self Portrait, by Charles Russell

The Story Teller, by Charles Russell

CHARLIE RUSSELL

TALE-TELLING COWBOY ARTIST

Lois V. Harris

PELICAN PUBLISHING COMPANY

GRETNA 2010

To my grandsons, Brandon and Jimmy Harris,
to follow their dreams,
and to Brent Trathen, who did

The word "Pelican" and the depiction of a pelican are trademarks
of Pelican Publishing Company, Inc., and are registered in the
U.S. Patent and Trademark Office.

Library of Congress Cataloging-in-Publication Data

Harris, Lois V.
  Charlie Russell : tale-telling cowboy artist / by Lois V. Harris. — 1st ed.
    p. cm.
  ISBN 978-1-58980-758-7 (alk. paper)
  1. Russell, Charles M. (Charles Marion), 1864-1926—Juvenile literature. 2.
Artists—United States—Biography—Juvenile literature. 3. West (U.S.)—In
art—Juvenile literature. I. Russell, Charles M. (Charles Marion), 1864-1926.
II. Title. III. Title: Tale-telling cowboy artist.
  N6537.R88H36 2010
  709.2—dc22
  [B]
                                                    2009039454

Printed in Singapore

Published by Pelican Publishing Company, Inc.
1000 Burmaster Street, Gretna, Louisiana 70053

St. Louis, steel engraving by Frederick Hawkins Piercy

CHARLIE RUSSELL

TALE-TELLING COWBOY ARTIST

Sometimes Charlie Russell played hooky from school. He sneaked down to the busy St. Louis, Missouri docks to hear frontier stories about gun-shooting bandits, grizzly bears, and hungry wolves. As gold seekers, fur traders, and pioneers stepped aboard paddleboats heading up the Missouri River, Charlie longed to go, too. The next day his teacher would always whip him for skipping school, but he kept dreaming of the West.

Russell residence

Charlie was born during the Civil War, on March 19, 1864, to Mary and Charles S. Russell in St. Louis. On his pony, he played "Settlers and Injuns" with his sister and four brothers.

Bear, by Charles Russell

His family owned a company that made bricks from clay. At the plant, Charlie dug small lumps of clay from the earth to make animal figures. The workmen came from England, Ireland, and Scotland. He copied their way of speaking and made his family laugh.

His teachers didn't think it was funny when he drew pictures instead of doing his schoolwork. Charlie liked history and adventure stories but hated math. He talked other boys into doing his homework and paid them with clay or wax figures.

Untitled (Horse Scratching Ear), by Charles Russell

Six Reins to Kingdom Come, by Charles Russell

When he was fifteen, Charlie announced he was going West. His parents got a job for him on a sheep ranch. They thought he would return after a summer of hard work. Charlie had other ideas.

In his suitcase, Charlie packed a box with pencils, brushes, watercolors, crayons, and a tin of beeswax for shaping small figures. He rode a train and a stagecoach over 1,800 miles to Montana Territory.

When Wagon Trails Were Dim, by Charles Russell

He passed tiny towns, lonely ranch houses, and cattle herds. Wagon trains rolled across the endless grassy plains toward the distant snow-covered mountains.

The Tenderfoot, by Charles Russell

In Helena, Indians wore colorful blankets and buckskin clothes. Cowboys on horseback galloped by, waving and yelling to friends. Men with guns played cards, cursed, and spit tobacco juice.

Charlie felt he belonged here. With money his parents had given him, he bought a wide-brimmed hat, a horse, bridle, saddle, and lasso and rode out to the sheep ranch.

Charlie Russell, by unidentified photographer

But instead of watching the sheep, he sketched. The sheep strayed, and the rancher fired him. "The sheep and I didn't get along well," said Charlie later.

Charlie left the ranch and sat by a river. His stomach rumbled. He had no job and not much money.

Jake Hoover, a trapper, rode up. After learning that Charlie had no place to go, he invited him to his mountain cabin. Charlie accepted right away.

The cabin sat in a grassy area that was "more green and beautiful than any man-made parks," said Charlie later.

Deer in Forest, by Charles Russell

The Exalted Ruler, by Charles Russell

Bears, deer, and elk wandered by.

And at night, wolves howled while Charlie sketched before a blazing fire, listening to Jake's stories.

Wolf With Bone, by Charles Russell

Charlie helped Jake sell or trade fresh meat to settlers. One day Jake advised him to get a good horse with the money he had earned. Charlie bought a pinto from the Blackfeet Indians and named him Monte.

"We don't exactly talk to each other," said Charlie, "but we sure savvy one another." They were friends for more than twenty-five years.

When I Was a Kid, by Charles Russell

When Charlie turned seventeen, he landed his first cowboy job. The other cowboys called him Kid Russell.

Under a great starry sky, Charlie ate bacon and beans cooked over a crackling campfire.

Laugh Kills Lonesome, by Charles Russell

Bronc to Breakfast, by Charles Russell

The men told stories, and he did too, especially funny ones about them. While speaking in his deep voice, Charlie drew pictures on tin, wood, boxes, playing cards, wagon covers—anything he could find. Other times, his long fingers swiftly shaped animal figures from beeswax.

Waiting for a Chinook (The Last of 5000), by Charles Russell

When Charlie was twenty-two, the long cold winter of 1886-87 blasted the West. Hundreds of thousands of cattle died. The animals couldn't paw away the snow and ice to eat the buried grass.

A worried cattleman wrote to Charlie's boss, asking how his herd was doing. As the wind whistled round the bunkhouse, Charlie drew a picture of a starving cow surrounded by wolves and wrote, "This is how it is."

The shocked cattleman sent copies of the picture around the country and to England. Now people called Charlie "The Cowboy Artist."

19

About this time, he visited Canada, where the Blood Indians taught him their sign language. The Bloods were one of the Plains Indian tribes living on the Western grasslands. These tribes spoke different languages but used the same hand gestures in order to understand each other. With his new skill, Charlie delighted the Bloods with stories. When he returned to Montana, signing brought him new Indian friends who shared stories about their people.

York, by Charles Russell

When the Land Belonged to God, by Charles Russell

In 1893, Charlie became a full-time artist. He never took an art lesson. Instead, he studied pictures in books and magazines and said, "Nature has been my teacher."

Going to a Christmas Ranch Party in the 1880s, by Charles Russell

Now and then Charlie sold or traded his artwork for grub or to pay bills. With no home of his own, Charlie lived with friends, telling stories and giving them his art. He said, "Good friends make the roughest trail easy."

Newlyweds Charlie and Nancy, by Elite Studio

In 1896, at age thirty-two, he married Nancy Cooper. She was eighteen, lively, and smart. Nancy started selling his art, and his pictures appeared in books, calendars, and magazines.

23

Charlie also wrote a magazine series of short chatty yarns. He put the best of them in his book, *Trails Plowed Under.*

In one story, he says, "Singin's a good thing around a herd . . . in the darkness it lets the cows know where you're at. If you ever woke up in the darkness an' found somebody—you didn't know who or what—loomin' up over you, it would startle you, but if this somebody is singin' or whistlin', it wouldn't scare you none."

A Dangerous Situation, by Charles Russell

24

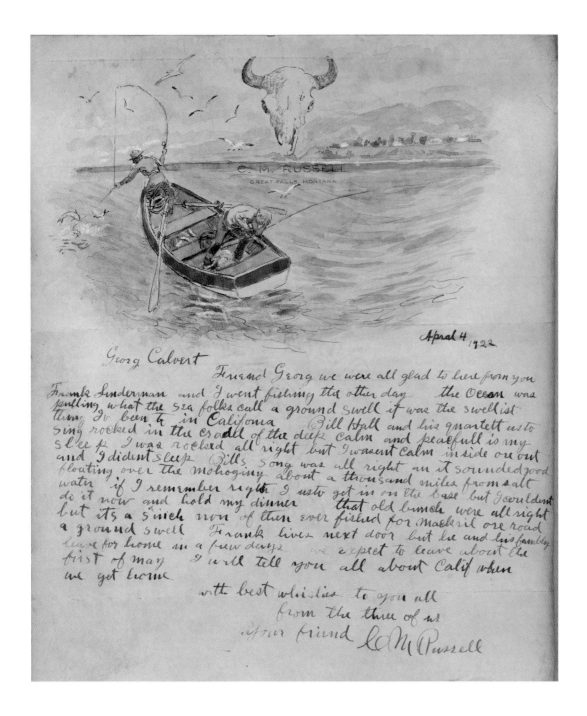

Letter to George Calvert, by Charles Russell

Drawing came easily to him but not writing. He said, "I'm one of the men that sweats when I write."

Even so, he sent his friends letters decorated with sketches.

After awhile, Nancy and Charlie had a house built for them and a barn for Monte. And next door was an art studio like his friend Jake's cabin. Charlie hung gifts from his friends on the wall. "That'll be a good shack for me," Charlie said. "The bunch can come visit, talk and smoke, while I paint."

Charles M. Russell on Horse, by A. O. Gregory

Charles Russell, by unidentified photographer

26

Roping a Prairie Wolf, by Charles Russell

Newspapers praised his art, and people collected it.

Some believed that the bronze sculptures made from his wax figures were better than his paintings.

Bronc Twister, by Charles Russell

In 1916 he and Nancy adopted a son, Jack. Charlie told many stories to him and to other children who gathered around him wherever he went.

On October 24, 1926, Charlie died suddenly at age sixty-two. A few months before, he wrote, "I lived to play and I'm playing yet."

Charlie and Jack, by unidentified photographer

Lewis and Clark Meeting Indians at Ross' Hole,
by Charles Russell

Charles M. Russell's love for the West echoes through time in his gift to us— lively artwork and writings, all telling the tales of the Old West. As he once wrote:

The west is dead my friend
But writers hold the seed
And what they sow
Will live and grow
Again to those that read

CREDITS

p. 1: *Self Portrait*, Charles Russell painting, watercolor on paper, Buffalo Bill Historical Center, Cody, Wyoming; Gift of Charles Ulrick and Josephine Bay Foundation, Inc., 98.60.

p. 2: *The Story Teller*, Charles Russell painting, watercolor on paper, Buffalo Bill Historical Center, Cody, Wyoming; Gift of William E. Weiss, 11.74.

p. 5: *St. Louis*, Frederick Hawkins Piercy steel engraving, BX 8673.41.P611r 1997, Americana Rare, *Route from Liverpool to Great Salt Lake Valley*, Franklin D. Richards, London, 1855, Courtesy L. Tom Perry Special Collections, Harold B. Lee Library, Brigham Young University, Provo, Utah.

p. 6: Residence of Chas. S. Russell Family. View of Right Flank. Oakhill Farm. 1875 [St. Louis, Missouri] [no date], Artist Unidentified, Lot 9, Box 1, F12.01, Montana Historical Society Research Center Photographic Archives, Helena, MT.

p. 7 top: *Bear*, Charles Russell, animal figurine, 1910s-1920s, Museum of the American West, Autry National Center of the American West, Los Angeles; 91.221.42.

p. 7 bottom: *Untitled (Horse Scratching Ear)*, Charles M. Russell, n.d., pencil, Joe De Yong/Richard J. Flood Collection, National Cowboy & Western Heritage Museum, Oklahoma City, Oklahoma, 1980.18.489.

p. 8: *Six Reins to Kingdom Come*, Charles M. Russell, Wax, Oil, 1901, Montana Historical Society Collection, X1972.01.01.

p. 9: *When Wagon Trails Were Dim*, Charles M. Russell, 1919, oil on canvas, Permanent Art Collection, National Cowboy & Western Heritage Museum, Oklahoma City, Oklahoma, 1975.020.0005.

p. 10: *The Tenderfoot*, Charles M. Russell, 1900, oil on canvas, Courtesy Sid Richardson Collection of Western Art, Fort Worth, Texas.

p. 11: Charles M. Russell [no date], Photographer Unidentified, Catalog # 944-689, Montana Historical Society Research Center Photographic Archives, Helena, MT.

p. 12: *Deer in Forest*, Charles M. Russell, 1917, oil on canvasboard, Courtesy Sid Richardson Collection of Western Art, Fort Worth, Texas.

p. 13: *The Exalted Ruler*, Charles M. Russell, oil on canvas, 1912, C. M. Russell Museum, Great Falls, Montana.

p. 14: *Wolf With Bone*, Charles M. Russell, bronze sculpture, courtesy of the R. W. Norton Art Gallery, Shreveport, Louisiana.

p. 15: *When I Was a Kid*, Charles M. Russell, 1905, watercolor on paper, courtesy of the Collection of Frederic G. and Ginger K. Renner, Paradise Valley, Arizona.

pp. 16-17: *Laugh Kills Lonesome*, Charles M. Russell, Oil on Canvas, 1925, Montana Historical Society, Mackay Collection, X1955.01.01.

p. 18: *Bronc to Breakfast*, Charles M. Russell, Watercolor, 1908, Montana Historical Society, Mackay Collection, X1952.01.06.

p. 19: *Waiting for a Chinook (The Last of 5000)*, Charles M. Russell, Watercolor, 1887. Used with permission from the Montana Stockgrowers Association, Helena, Montana.

p. 20: *York*, Charles M. Russell, Watercolor, 1908, Courtesy of the Montana Historical Society, X1909.01.01, Photography by John Reddy, 2000.

p. 21: *When the Land Belonged to God*, Charles M. Russell, Oil, 1914, Montana Historical Society Collection, X1977.01.01, Photography by John Reddy, 1998.

p. 22: *Going to a Christmas Ranch Party in the 1880s*, Charles M. Russell, watercolor, 1908, C. M. Russell Museum, Great Falls, Montana.

p. 23: Charles Russell & wife Nancy. 1896, Photograph by Elite Studio, Great Falls, Catalog # 944-674, Montana Historical Society Research Center Photographic Archives, Helena, MT.

p. 24: *A Dangerous Situation*, Charles Marion Russell (1864-1926), oil on wood panel, 1897, 12 x 18 3/8 inches, Stark Museum of Art, Orange, Texas, 31.11.1.

p. 25: *Letter to George Calvert*, Charles M. Russell, watercolor, pen and ink, April 4, 1922, C. M. Russell Museum, Great Falls, Montana.

p. 26 top: *Charles M. Russell on Horse*, A. O. Gregory, 1908, photograph, Joe De Yong/Richard J. Flood Collection, National Cowboy & Western Heritage Museum, Oklahoma City, Oklahoma, 1980.18.641.6.

p. 26 bottom: Charles M. Russell painting "Whose Meat." Log cabin studio. Great Falls, MT. 1914, Photographer Unidentified, Catalog # 944-708, Montana Historical Society Research Center Photographic Archives, Helena, MT.

p. 27: *Roping a Prairie Wolf*, Charles Marion Russell, 1904, watercolor and gouache on artist board, Collection Palm Springs Art Museum, Gift of Mrs. Virginia H. Mayo Daniger.

p. 28: *Bronc Twister*, Charles M. Russell, bronze sculpture, courtesy of the R. W. Norton Art Gallery, Shreveport, Louisiana.

p. 29: Charles M. Russell and adopted son Jack [no date], Photographer Unidentified, Catalog # 944-679, Montana Historical Society Research Center Photographic Archives, Helena, MT.

p. 30: *Lewis and Clark Meeting Indians at Ross' Hole*, Charles M. Russell, Oil on Canvas, 1912, Mural in State of Montana Capitol, Montana Historical Society Collection, X1912.06.01, Photograph by Don Beatty, 1999.